my Joy! Kid

with

ith love from:

Contents:

Christian Media Publishing,
PO Box 4502, Durbanville, 7551
www.christianmediapublishing.com

Author: Ewald van Rensburg

Illustrations, Design & Layout: Lilani Brits

Publishing Project Manager: Noeline N Neumann

Reg No 2010/008573/07

Text: Maranatha Publishing: Used by kind agreement.

Printed in Malaysia through PrettyInPress Productions.
First edition, first printing 2013

ISBN 978-1-920593-42-1

CMP-kids books have been developed with your child's
developmental phases and unique temperament in mind.
For a full explanation of the **unique temperament** and **developmental phases**
icons visit the CMP website **www.cmpublishing.co.za**

about friendship

Written by Ewald van Rensburg
Illustrations by Lilani Brits

Kids celebrate being a good friend!

christian media publishing **Kids**

pointing children in the **right direction**

1. David and Jonathan

(1 Samuel 20)

After he killed Goliath, David went to live with King Saul. All the Israelites liked David a lot because he had beaten Goliath; and also because he wrote beautiful songs. Saul was very jealous of David.

A wonderful thing happened, David and Saul's son, Jonathan, became best friends. They played together every day and loved each other very much.

Jonathan heard that his father, Saul, wanted to kill David. So he helped David escape from Saul.

Come, let's pray together:

Lord, thank You for all my friends.
Amen

Friends always help each other.

2. Lazarus

(John 11:1-44)

Jesus' friends, Martha, Mary and their brother Lazarus, lived in a small village called Bethany, near Jerusalem.

One day Lazarus became very sick. Martha and Mary sent someone to tell Jesus.

Sadly Jesus arrived at their house too late; Lazarus had died four days earlier. Jesus saw how sad Martha and Mary were. He started crying too, because He also loved Lazarus.

Jesus went with the sisters to Lazarus' grave. He started crying again, and said "Lazarus, come out!"

Then Lazarus came walking out of his grave! Everyone was so happy to see him alive again.

Come, let's pray together:

Jesus, thank You that You comfort me when I am sad. Amen

3. Jesus walks with two friends
(Luke 24:13-35)

Two of Jesus' friends were walking to their village, Emmaus. They were talking about Jesus' death. A man came along and started walking with them. It was Jesus.

The men didn't recognise Him because they were so sad that Jesus had died. Jesus talked to them about the Scriptures.

When they got home they invited Him to have supper with them.

As He broke the bread and thanked God for it, they saw it was Jesus! Then Jesus went away.

The two friends rushed to tell the other disciples: "Jesus is alive! We saw Him with our own eyes!"

Come, let's pray together:

Jesus, I'm so glad You are alive. Thank You for telling me about it in the Bible. Amen

Jesus has beaten death.

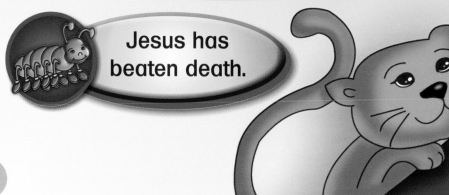

4. A story about fishing

(John 21:1-13)

Peter and the other disciples had been out fishing in their boat all night - but they couldn't catch any fish. When they rowed back in their empty boat, Jesus was waiting for them on the shore. They didn't recognise Him.

He said to them, "Throw your nets out again!" This time they caught a lot of fish. Then John shouted, "It's Jesus!" and Peter dived into the sea and swam quickly to the shore.

When the disciples reached the shore,
Jesus had already made a breakfast
of fish and bread for them. Then He sat
down and ate with them.

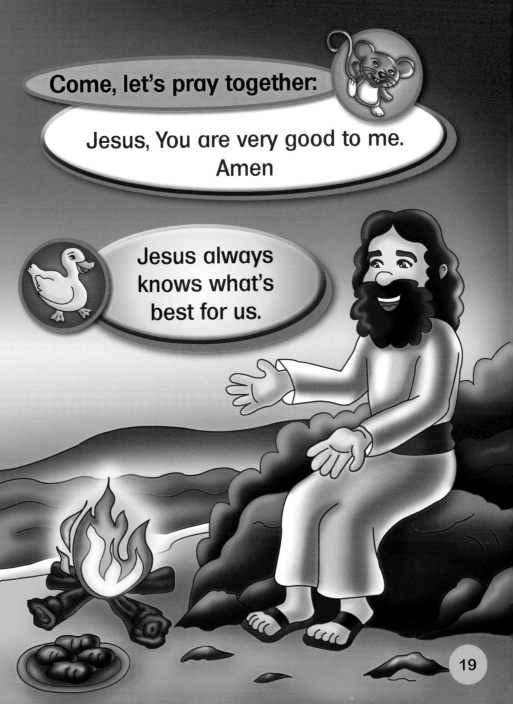

5. Peter, John and a crippled man (Acts 3:1-26)

One day, Peter and John saw a crippled man begging near the temple. He asked them for some money.
Peter said to him, "Look at us."
The man looked at them because he hoped they were going to give him something. "I have no money; but I will give you what I have. In the name of Jesus, stand up and walk!" said Peter.

At once the man stood up and began walking. He jumped up and down because he was so happy! He couldn't stop saying thank You to God.

Come, let's pray together:

Jesus, thank You that You use me to help other people every day.
Amen

Children of God always help people in trouble.

Faith Icon

The formation of faith is indeed unique to each child; there are however general characteristics that apply to all children. There are three main ways in which children develop faith:

- Parents regularly reading the Bible, telling Bible and other faith based stories, praying together and doing faith building activities with their children (such as the ones found in this book).
- Children ask questions – parents need to take these questions seriously and answer them according to the child's level of understanding.
- Children follow the example of those caring for them.

Emotional Intelligence Icon

We experience emotions long before we learn the language that enables us to express how we are feeling. Therefore it is important for children to be taught how to verbalise what they are feeling. Use the illustrations accompanying the stories and ask your child how they think the people or animals in the picture feel. This helps them become aware of their own emotions as well as those of others. It provides a learning opportunity where the child can learn appropriate words to express how they are feeling.

Reading Icon

A wonderful world opens up for your child when they start learning to read. Enjoy every moment of this exciting adventure with your child. Let them sit on your lap where they can be comfortable and feel safe and secure. Open the book holding it so that you can both see the pages. Read clearly and with enthusiasm. As you know you can read the same story over and over. Point out where you are reading with your finger as you go along. This will help your child to begin to see the relationship between letters, sounds, words and their meaning. Encourage your child's attempts at reading – even if it sounds like gibberish.

Listening Skills Icon

Listening is an important learning and developmental skill. You can help develop this skill in your child by encouraging them to listen attentively, and understand what they are hearing. Let them look at the illustrations and then use their imagination to tell the story back to you in their own words. You can also encourage them to do this by asking questions relating to the story. Yet another way is to leave out words from a story the child knows well and let them fill in the missing words.

Vocabulary Icon

Use every opportunity to build your child's vocabulary – this is a lifelong gift that you are giving to them. Start with everyday objects and people in the illustrations in books. Point at the picture, say the word, form a short sentence using the word. Repeat it again and then let your child say the word. Try to use the word in another context – if there is a tent in the picture you are looking at then say: we sleep in a tent when we go camping.

Numeracy Skills Icon

It is important for your child to develop numeracy skills. Play simple games such as: "How many ducks are there in the picture? If we add two more ducks how many are there now? Then if three fly away? (use your fingers to illustrate this) How many are left?" They also need to recognise the shape of numbers – cut large numbers from cardboard – let your child play with these – place the numbers in order forming a line from one to ten.